GEO
KIDS

Exploring The

By
Holly Duhig

SEASHORE

BookLife
PUBLISHING

ISBN: 978-1-78637-437-0

Written by:
Holly Duhig

©2019
BookLife Publishing
King's Lynn
Norfolk PE30 4LS
All rights reserved.
Printed in Malaysia.

Edited by:
Emilie Dufresne

Designed by:
Gareth Liddington

A catalogue record for this book is available from the British Library.

CONTENTS

Page 4	Exploring the Seashore
Page 6	Playing in the Sand!
Page 8	Sandy Habitats
Page 10	Rock Pools!
Page 12	Rock Pool Habitats
Page 14	Picnic on the Sand Dunes!
Page 16	What Are Sand Dunes?
Page 18	Crab Fishing!
Page 20	Crabs
Page 22	Fish and Chips!
Page 24	Glossary and Index

Words that look like **this** can be found in the glossary on page 24.

EXPLORING THE SEASHORE

My name is Max and I live near a beach. I love exploring the seashore! It is only a short walk from my house to the beach.

At school, we are learning all about different **environments**. We are doing a project on an environment of our choice. I'm doing my project on the seashore!

Exploring The
SEASHORE

GEO KIDS

N
E

Max Thatcher's Seashore Project

I love the beach all year round — in summer when it's hot and windy days too!

PLAYING IN THE SAND!

Sometimes I build a moat around my sandcastle so that the water from the sea flows into it.

I always take my bucket and spade with me when we go to the beach. That way I can dig holes and build sandcastles.

I also love drawing in the sand. Sometimes I write my name and other times I draw pictures. They all get washed away by the waves in the end.

I use the end of my fishing net to draw with, but you can use driftwood too.

SANDY HABITATS

Lugworm

A habitat is an animal's home.

Castings!

When I was playing in the sand, I noticed lots of squiggly things and I wanted to find out more about them. The squiggles are made by lugworms and they are actually lugworm castings (poo!).

8

The lugworms eat the sand that they burrow through. Their burrows are U-shaped. This means they can eat at one end of the burrow and poo at the other!

Lugworm Burrows

ROCK POOLS!

Rock pools are really fun to explore. Lots of little creatures live in them. I always wear wellies to explore rock pools because there are lots of sharp things, like shells, that can hurt your feet.

I also take a fishing net and a bucket with me. I scoop up the things I find in the fishing net and put them in my bucket to get a closer look.

Sometimes I just use my hands!

ROCK POOL HABITATS

I saw lots of interesting things in the rock pools. Some of the creatures I saw were:

Crab

If starfish lose a limb they can grow a new one. It can take nearly a year for it to grow back.

Starfish

Mussel

I also found seaweed in the rock pools. There are over 10,000 different species of seaweed. Some seaweed is green but some is red or even brown.

Some seaweed has bubbles on it that you can pop!

PICNIC ON THE SAND DUNES!

Some beaches have sand dunes. They are really fun to play in. You can jump off them, roll down them or play hide and seek in the long grass.

We always take a picnic with us when we go to the beach. The sand dunes are the perfect place to sit and eat it. We have jam sandwiches, crisps, apples, oranges and yoghurts in our picnic.

WHAT ARE SAND DUNES?

Sand in the Wind

Sand dunes are hills of sand that you find at the beach. You normally have to climb over them to get to the flat part of the beach. They are made from wind blowing sand from the beach towards the land.

After a while, the sand builds up and becomes a dune. The bigger the dunes get, the more sand they trap. Sometimes plants, like grasses, start growing on sand dunes.

The plant's roots hold the sand in one place and trap even more sand.

CRAB FISHING!

We use all sorts of bait to catch the crabs. They really like fish and bacon!

When we go to the seashore, we like to go crab fishing. We normally fish for crabs from the **seafront** when the **tide** is high.

To go crab fishing you need a net (that's where you put the bait), a long crabbing line and weights so that your net doesn't just float on top of the water.

CRABS

After going crab fishing, I wanted to find out as much as I could about crabs.

Pea Crab

Japanese Spider Crab

Crabs can be really big or really small. The smallest crab is the pea crab; it is only 6-11 millimetres wide. The biggest crab is the Japanese spider crab which is around 4 metres wide.

Crabs are crustaceans. This means they have hard shells, lots of legs and live underwater. Crabs have ten legs which they use to walk sideways.

FISH AND CHIPS!

I've had so much fun exploring the seashore!
I've learnt lots about the animals and plants that
live in the sea and on the beach. It will soon be
time to go home but there's still one thing left to do…

Fish and Chips!

GLOSSARY

driftwood	pieces of wood which are floating on the sea or have been washed ashore
environments	needs to be changed to 'the areas in which a human, animal or plant lives
moat	a deep, wide ditch surrounding a castle that is usually filled with water
seafront	the part of a town on the coast and next to the sea
tide	the rising and falling of sea levels
roots	the part of a plant that grows underground and collects water and nutrients
species	a group of very similar animals or plants that are capable of producing young together
limb	the arm, leg or wing of an animal

INDEX

bucket 6, 11

burrows 9

crabs 12, 18-21

driftwood 7

fishing net 7, 11, 19

lugworms 8-9

mussels 12

plants 17, 22

sandcastles 6

seaweed 13

tide 18

wind 16